# LIFE

# Holy Lands

## One Place Three Faiths

# Judaism

It is the oldest of the three great monotheistic religions. Judaism's view of history, as rendered in the Torah some 2,600 years ago, provided a basis for Christianity and, later, Islam. The Israelite leader Moses, who received the Lord's laws atop Mount Sinai—perhaps this very summit on the Sinai Peninsula—is a revered prophet in all three faiths.

# LIFE
# Holy Lands

## One Place Three Faiths

# Christianity

In Israel, 2,000 years ago, a child was born to a Jewish couple. Jesus grew to be a charismatic preacher, gathering disciples as he went. This Son of God performed miracles, they said: raising the dead, calming these waters of Galilee. Jerusalem's authorities, perceiving a threat, had Jesus executed. His followers, taking up the cross, built the world's largest religion in his name.

# LIFE
# Holy Lands

**One Place** Three Faiths

# Islam

More than 1,300 years ago, a man in Mecca was visited by the archangel
Gabriel and received an extraordinary gift: the word from Allah, the one God.
Muhammad, according to Muslims, was the prophet presaged by Moses,
and Muhammad's book, the Koran, represented the ultimate truth. Taking
his message across the desert to Medina, near these hills, he created Islam.

# LIFE
# Holy Lands

**One Place** Three Faiths

**Managing Editor** Robert Sullivan
**Director of Photography** Barbara Baker Burrows
**Creative Director** Ian Denning;
Mimi Park (2012 edition)
**Executive Editor** Robert Andreas
**Deputy Picture Editor** Christina Lieberman
**Associate Picture Editor** Vivette Porges
**Senior Reporter** Hildegard Anderson
**Writer/Reporters** Lauren Nathan;
Michelle DuPré, Amy Lennard Goehner
(2012 edition)
**Copy Editors** J.C. Choi (Chief); Stacy Sabraw;
Barbara Gogan, Parlan McGaw (2012 edition)
**Production Manager** Michael Roseman
**Picture Research** Lauren Steel
**Photo Assistants** Joshua Colow;
Sarah Cates (2012 edition)
**Consulting Picture Editors**
Suzanne Hodgart (London); Mimi Murphy (Rome);
Tala Skari (Paris)

**Editorial Director** Stephen Koepp
**Editorial Operations Director** Michael Q. Bullerdick

**Editorial Operations** Richard K. Prue (Director),
Brian Fellows (Manager), Richard Shaffer
(Production), Keith Aurelio, Charlotte Coco,
Kevin Hart, Mert Kerimoglu, Rosalie Khan,
Patricia Koh, Marco Lau, Brian Mai, Po Fung Ng,
Rudi Papiri, Robert Pizaro, Barry Pribula,
Clara Renauro, Katy Saunders, Hia Tan,
Vaune Trachtman

**Time Home Entertainment**

**Publisher** Jim Childs
**Vice President, Business Development & Strategy**
Steven Sandonato
**Executive Director, Marketing Services** Carol Pittard
**Executive Director, Retail & Special Sales** Tom Mifsud
**Executive Publishing Director** Joy Butts
**Director, Bookazine Development & Marketing**
Laura Adam
**Finance Director** Glenn Buonocore
**Associate Publishing Director** Megan Pearlman
**Assistant General Counsel** Helen Wan
**Assistant Director, Special Sales** Ilene Schreider
**Book Production Manager** Suzanne Janso
**Design & Prepress Manager** Anne-Michelle Gallero
**Brand Manager** Roshni Patel
**Associate Prepress Manager** Alex Voznesenskiy
**Assistant Brand Manager** Stephanie Braga

**Special thanks:** Christine Austin, Katherine Barnet,
Jeremy Biloon, Susan Chodakiewicz, Rose Cirrincione,
Lauren Hall Clark, Jacqueline Fitzgerald, Christine Font,
Jenna Goldberg, Hillary Hirsch, David Kahn,
Amy Mangus, Robert Marasco, Kimberly Marshall,
Amy Migliaccio, Nina Mistry, Dave Rozzelle,
Ricardo Santiago, Adriana Tierno, Vanessa Wu

ISBN 10: 1-60320-235-8
ISBN 13: 978-1-60320-235-0
Library of Congress Control Number: 2012947534

"LIFE" is a registered trademark of Time Inc.

We welcome your comments and suggestions
about LIFE Books. Please write to us at:
LIFE Books, Attention: Book Editors, PO Box 11016,
Des Moines, IA 50336-1016

If you would like to order any of our hardcover
Collector's Edition books, please call us at
1-800-327-6388 (Monday through Friday,
7:00 a.m.–8:00 p.m. or Saturday,
7:00 a.m.–6:00 p.m. Central Time).

# Jerusalem

**In Hebrew it is Yerushalayim, in Arabic Bayt al-Muqaddas. It is 3,800 years old, and if it has been controlled politically by Israel since 1967, it remains a spiritual stronghold of three great religions: Judaism, Christianity and Islam. A place of prophets, martyrs, tension and turmoil, Jerusalem holds the promise of life eternal—and the lurking prospect of sudden death.**

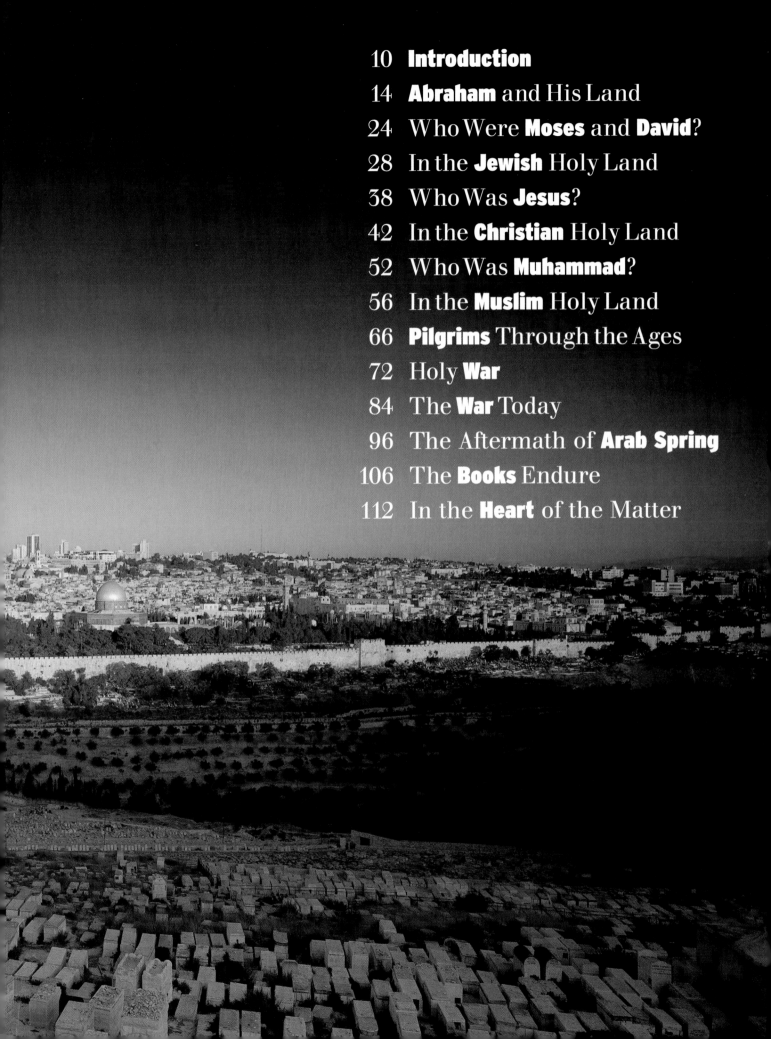

# One Place Three Faiths

When we first published *Holy Lands* a decade ago, there was every evident reason for such a book. The events of 9/11 only months earlier had caused all to ask questions: What is the difference between radical Islam and devout Islam? Where do tensions lie among the three great monotheistic religions: Islam, Christianity and Judaism? Are their quarrels strictly theological or cultural or both? Where can we all find agreement? Coexistence? What part of our faith-based heritage is shared? Whence did this all spring? Where did it start? That last question, at least, was easy to answer, and we went to the Middle East.

Ten years on, there is every evident reason to revisit the part of the world—its history, both ancient and current—where all of this did indeed start. Three of the world's great religions call various sites in the region "holy," all three have origin narratives based there, and Islam and Judaism still call large areas within that region home. As for Christianity: LIFE pointed out in 2002 that Pope John Paul's pilgrimage to the holy land at the dawn of the new millennium (in his Church's

Right: In Libya during the Arab Spring, so-called "Green Books," which delineate the political philosophy of Muammar Gadhafi—the despotic ruler's equivalent of Mao's "Little Red Book"—are burned. Below: In Al Galaa Park in Damascus, a boy signs a scroll honoring martyrs of the uprisings in Syria. He and other young people have gathered for a "Stand in Silent Grief" protest, and their petition reads in part, "We are here today to ask all Syrians to consider this moment as the end of our sadness and to make it a point for a beginning to work together to end the flow of Syrian blood." Their eloquent and heartfelt protest has as yet had minimal effect.

THOMAS DWORZAK/MAGNUM

reckoning of the calendar) was politely received by his hosts, but only served to point up that Christianity's influence in the land of Christ's birth has all but evaporated. The pope was preaching in a land of many Christian relics and sites but, in the modern day, precious few Christians. A 1,300-year rise of Islam had already eroded the Christian population among Arabs before the 20th century, and then as troubles between Muslims and Jews intensified, the erosion accelerated. In 1946, 13 percent of Palestine was Christian; by 2000, the figure for the region was a minuscule 2.1 percent. As Christians have absented themselves, there have been consequences, an obvious one being that warring parties are left to sort things out for themselves with no mediating voice. (That sentence is written with full knowledge that Catholics did plenty of warring themselves in the holy land during the so-called Crusades.) In his book *The Body and the Blood,* historian Charles M. Sennott writes: "If the Christians disappear, the Middle East will become that much more vulnerable to this embittered dichotomy."

That dichotomy has been reflected in the last decade by continuous skirmishes, regular incidents of suicide warfare, bombs being lobbed into and out of Israel. In the past two years came the twist that led us at LIFE Books to decide to reissue *Holy Lands* and to update it. With the rise of the Internet and the cameraphone as social weaponry, the embittered class in several parts of the Arab world began to coalesce and rise up. It redirected its complaints to its own various authoritarian regimes. Some of these dictatorial governments have been toppled, notably those in Egypt and Libya, and these events will be reviewed in our book's new penultimate chapter. Some longstanding governments continue to exert authority even as we go to press with this new edition. As these words are being typed, Syria's dictatorial president, Bashar al-Assad, remains in power and defiant, and the United Nations is saying that 100,000 Syrians fled the country in August 2012, a marked acceleration of an exodus caused by 18 months of conflict that has wreaked, according to the new United Nations–Arab League envoy Lakhdar Brahimi, a "staggering . . . catastrophic" death toll, estimated by some watchdog groups as north of 25,000 people, two thirds of them civilians. The situation, Brahimi warned, was "deteriorating steadily."

The term *Arab Spring* bears connotations of populism, liberation and freedom, but as we consider the final fate of Libya's Muammar Gadhafi, the September 2012 murder of U.S. ambassador to Libya Chris Stevens and three other Americans, and the ongoing situation in Syria, we realize that this is, in some places, true war, and it is far from settled.

When it finally *is* sorted out—in a year, a decade or a century, if ever—what will that mean for the holy land? Israel is, in the short term (and probably the long), wary. When this year's voting results in Egypt put a Muslim Brotherhood candidate, Mohamed Morsy, in the president's chair after he defeated all secular rivals, there was grave concern. The Jewish state

fears that a proliferation of Islamist regimes throughout the region will only add fuel to the powerful religious aspect that informs all political arguments in the region. War between nations is always dangerous and a thing to be feared. Holy war between nations can be more dangerous by half.

So, here and now, we revise a book that has from the first sought to lend historical context to a complicated situation. That situation has been newly complicated in ways that never could have been presaged when the principal questions were

"Who's this Osama bin Laden?" and "What is al-Qaeda?" He has been killed, and whether his organization's influence in the Arab Spring has been somewhat significant, marginal or altogether nonexistent is debated today by social scientists. What is clear, however: The attacks of September 11, 2001, evoked connections to the holy land; and today's revolutionary spirit in the streets of Cairo and Tripoli—and, day after day, even in the streets of Damascus—has already reshaped the holy land. It is time to take another look.

Above: In a holy land scene that resembles Leonardo's "Last Supper," protestors who have been sleeping by barricades at the edge of Cairo's Tahrir Square signal victory after hearing of the resignation of Egyptian president Hosni Mubarak. Top right: In a celebrated gesture during his 2000 pilgrimage to the holy land, Pope John Paul II inserts into Jerusalem's Western Wall an apology for Christian misdeeds. Bottom: Two years later in that city, a third depiction of hope as Shani Batut (left), an 8-year-old Israeli, plays with Rada Derhy, a 10-year-old Palestinian, at a summer camp for 160 children that aims to foster understanding. It needs to be noted: Two weeks after this picture is made, a bomb is detonated in the campus cafeteria, killing seven. None of the children attending camp are physically harmed. But whatever lessons they were being taught, and whatever message their friendship sent, are buffeted, along with the summer calm.

It was at the Dead Sea that Sodom and Gomorrah fell. Lot, the nephew of Abraham, escaped, but his disobedient wife was turned into a pillar of salt. Some say this outcropping is Lot's wife.

# Abraham and His Land

He, as much as any this side of the supreme deity, belongs to them all. The shared beliefs of Judaism, Christianity and Islam include a single god, Adam and Eve, and a common roster of holy people—most importantly, Abraham.

The reasons for contemplating the holy lands of Judaism, Christianity and Islam at this time are evident. In a region forever plagued by territorial disputes, the recent heightened violence between Arabs and Jews—punctuated in 2002 by a horrific series of suicide bombings, cross-border attacks and now the Arab Spring—begs for an understanding of the roots of conflict. The fruitlessness of Pope John Paul II's pilgrimages to Jordan and Israel just over a decade ago, during which he apologized for past Roman Catholic misdeeds against other religions and pleaded for ecumenical compassion among all faiths, brings into question what influence Christianity retains in the land of Christ's birth.

And for Americans, there is, of course, September 11 and its aftermath. Radical Islamists said forcefully that the events of that day were about religion, about Western infidels transgressing on sacred soil in Saudi Arabia, about Muhammad's true teachings, about the need for global jihad. What did the message of September 11 really have to do with Islam, and how does that apply to what's going on week by week, day by day, hour by hour, in Jerusalem, Bethlehem, Hebron, Ramallah and, indeed, Riyadh, Rome, Washington, D.C.? And now, what does the Arab Spring of 2010–2012 mean?

The complexity of the equation is daunting, and certainly some answers cannot be known. For example, What is the difference between the devout believer, the fundamentalist and the radical? Through whose eyes are we looking when we make that determination?

There are things we cannot fathom and things that will have a different cast tomorrow than today. Nevertheless it is worthwhile to seek a basic understanding of the faiths involved: where they came from, their shared place, their shared history, some of their shared traditions, their different hopes and dreams for the future of their holy land. In assessing the Middle East today, it's not unreasonable to conclude that Judaism, Christianity and Islam are as different as the moon, the stars and the planets, and as antagonistic as dogs and cats. In deep history, however, nothing is further from

**Three views of Abraham's test: In an 18th century Jewish painting (below) and a Rembrandt from the 17th century, Abraham prepares to slay Isaac. In a Turkish illustration, circa 1583, he raises his knife to Ishmael. The Koran does not specify which son God asked Abraham to sacrifice, but Muslims consider Ishmael to be the designee and Mecca, rather than Jerusalem, the site.**

progenitors in all three faiths (even if Christianity is alone in teaching that their original sin had to be redeemed by Christ's crucifixion).

But while freely admitting that there is no way to address this topic in a rigorously secular manner, it is most useful to begin with a historical human being (who may or may not have existed; proving him is impossible) named Abraham.

Or Abram, as he appears in the earliest citations. These are in Genesis, in both the Hebrew and Christian Bibles, documents whose early chapters are also shared tradition with Islam. (The Koran, Islam's holy text as composed by Muhammad in the 7th century A.D., cites and sanctions many biblical characters and stories; until the time of Abraham, it is in general accord with biblical accounts of how things went.) According to Genesis, "Abram," a name referring to "father love" or an exaltation of the father, was one of Noah's 10th-generation descendants and was born in the Mesopotamian city of Ur (today, in the most prominent theory, Ur is Iraq's Tall al-Muqayyar, 200 miles southeast of Baghdad). In 2000, John Paul II

the truth. In deep history, they are one.

This argument could start with Yahweh or God or Allah, the single sacred being who is the heart and soul of all three religions. Before the rise of Judaism, Christianity and Islam, it was deviant thought that there was not a plurality of gods but, rather, one supreme being. Today, by contrast, more than half the planet adheres to a one-god theology, with 2 billion Christians, perhaps 1.5 billion Muslims and approximately 15 million Jews outnumbering the followers of pantheistic religions.

So this argument could start with God, or it could begin with Adam and Eve, humanity's

DAVID LEES

SATELLITE PHOTOGRAPH: PHOTO RESEARCHERS

**Excavations near Ur have revealed a city dating from circa 2000 B.C.—approximately the time of Abraham. From what was then a port on the Persian Gulf (Ur is now inland), Abraham went forth.**

*Mediterranean Sea*

Zoan

Cairo

E G Y P T

Nile

tried desperately to add Ur to his itinerary and said at one point that no Christian's Holy Land pilgrimage could be complete without a visit to Abraham's birthplace, but the Pope was rebuffed by Saddam Hussein.

According to the Bible's genealogies, and other historical writings measured against modern archaeological finds, it seems probable that Abraham, if he existed at all, lived sometime between 2100 and 1500 B.C. This was not a godless age in places such as Ur; it was a multi-god age. How Abram's thinking evolved to monotheism—and thereby put him in position to become the first patriarch of both the people of Israel and the Arabs—is speculative. Most of Ur looked up to a moon god named Sin, but Abram would be different.

According to scripture, his clan was migratory even before God gave Abram instructions to travel yet farther, and because of who he would become in the theologies of great religions, every step he and his people took served to sanctify holy ground. First they went west from Ur to Haran, between the Tigris and Euphrates rivers in northern Mesopotamia. Haran, which today is in Turkey, was a site of pilgrimage for Sin worshipers, and so an expected destination for citizens from Ur.

Abram's father, Terah, died in Haran at the age of 205, says the Bible. The good genes of his family would prove essential in the Abraham story, as will shortly be evident.

Abram's caravan, which included not only his wife Sarai but his biblically famous nephew Lot, went west again and forded the Euphrates, perhaps at Carchemish. Nayrab, near Aleppo, was another Sin city, and probably a stopping point. As new fields offered new opportunities of fortune to the itinerant shepherds, the journey continued: Damascus (probably), Shechem, Bethel (now Baytin, north of Jerusalem), southwest to Egypt and then back to the oaks of Mamre, which, according to Genesis, "are at Hebron." According to modern knowledge, they were a mile and a half northwest of Hebron, at a place now called Ramat al-Khalil, Arabic for "Heights of the Friend," Allah's friend being Abram. Amidst the oaks of Mamre, events of significance transpired, leading to narratives that would change the world.

Lot and his family were attacked, and Abram leapt into action, speeding northeast from Mamre to save him, showing a warrior instinct in one who theretofore was largely pacifist. This enlarges his character but does not fundamentally change his role, his

TURKEY

CYPRUS

Carchemish  Haran

Aleppo

Hamath

S Y R I A

Euphrates

Tigris

Mari

Beirut

LEBANON

Damascus

ISRAEL

Bethel

Jerusalem

Ammad

Hebron

Dead
Sea

Sodom and Gomorrah

J O R D A N

I R A Q

Baghdad

Babylon

Erech

Ur

I R A N

Ancient Coastline

Basra

KUWAIT

Kuwait

Persian
Gulf

S A U D I

A R A B I A

Red
Sea

## The Path of Abraham

It was at the behest of God that Abraham and his
people made the journey from their native land of
Mesopotamia into Canaan, which lay between Syria and
Egypt. In following Abraham's footsteps today, it is
evident that the patriarch's progress passes through
countries that have evolved in quite different ways.
From Iraq the route wends through Syria, Turkey and
Jordan before crossing and recrossing Israel, the West
Bank and the Sinai. This migration changed history.

Abraham's Path ⟵          Ancient City ○ Babylon

Modern Border ——          Modern City ○ Baghdad

DENIS WAUGH

**He was a city kid who became part of a nomadic caravan. In crossing what is now Judea, Abraham and his fellow shepherds would seek out fields with some fertility in the vast, arid desert.**

being. What did transform him—and, thus, every-thing—was the call from God to forsake his old country and to found a new nation in Canaan, between Mesopotamia and Egypt. If Abram took up this considerable task, he would be blessed with many offspring, and his "seed" would inherit what he surveyed. God pledged to Abram that if his people remained faithful, then Canaan, which included the modern Palestine, would be their "everlasting possession [Gen. 17:4–9]."

To this rough point in time, the Bible and the Koran do not vigorously disagree. Genesis and Muhammad's account of Allah's words in the Koran are in basic accord about who Abram was and what was promised to him. It is with the man's sons that the stories diverge.

Abram was 75 years old when he entered into his covenant with God, who in a later vision certi-fied the agreement by changing Abram's name to Abraham, meaning "Father of many nations." In the immediate aftermath of the first revelation, Abraham and Sarah, as she was renamed, remained childless, and what might come of the communication with God was uncertain. Sarah lent her Egyptian handmaiden, Hagar, to Abraham that she might bear him a child. This boy was Ishmael.

God continued to talk with Abraham; their debate about Sodom and Gomorrah, with Abraham urging leniency for the sinful cities, was a notable dialogue. (God, while moved by Abraham's argu-ments, destroyed the wicked citadels, though he spared Lot, who at the time was living in Sodom.) When Abraham was 99, God pledged him a son with Sarah. A year later she bore Isaac.

When she became a mother, Sarah insisted that her husband banish Hagar and Ishmael from his community, and Abraham obeyed. To greatly simplify the latter chapters of Abraham's story: In Genesis, God tests Abraham's faith by asking him to sacrifice Isaac. Abraham is on the verge of doing so atop Mount Moriah when God stays his hand, provides a ram as a substitute sacrifice and allows Isaac to grow, prosper and, through his son

**Above and below: Jews honor their heritage at the Tomb of the Patriarchs in Hebron, where Abraham, Sarah, and Isaac and his son Jacob are said to rest. Opposite: Abraham's failure to sway God is memorialized in this desolate land on the Dead Sea where it is said that Sodom and Gomorrah lie buried.**

Jacob (who will be called Israel), to found the Jewish nation in Palestine. According to Islam, it was Ishmael who was nearly sacrificed. His many offspring settled on the site of the future Mecca, where they flourished, spreading across the Arab world: the Muslims.

Abraham died at the age of 175 and was buried beside his wife in the Cave of Machpelah east of Mamre, which is today in the West Bank.

So Abraham was indeed the patriarch of many nations built beneath two overarching theologies: Judaism and Islam. As for his place in the Christian world, John Paul's high regard for the prophet is indicative. Abraham is cited 72 times in the New Testament, more than any Old Testament figure save Moses, and always with the utmost respect. No less an authority than St. Paul, in ardent admiration of Abraham's righteousness and pristine faith, speaks of him as "the father of us all [Rom. 4:16]."

The great religious saga in the Middle East starts with him, with Abraham. Where it will lead, we still do not know.

To Jews he is Moshe Rabbenu (Moses, Our Teacher), lawgiver, hero above all heroes; to Christians he is a model of faith; to Muslims, Musa is the first prophet to herald the coming of Muhammad. For Christians and Muslims, subsequent leaders Jesus and Muhammad delivered modified teachings that took precedence, but for Jews, whose Messiah is yet to come, Moses remains preeminent. "The most solitary and most powerful hero in biblical history," Elie Wiesel called Moses. "After him, nothing else was the same again."

He is said to have lived 3,200 years ago, in the time of Egyptian pharaoh Ramses II. Proving his existence has, as with Abraham, been impossible. Some scholars point out that several chapters in the Moses saga, beginning with the story of a baby in an ark woven of reeds, are similar to older Mesopotamian and Egyptian legends. So what? Even if Moses or aspects of him were borrowed, there are in the story entirely original philosophies. And, at its end, a revolutionary moral. Moses certainly seems real, and the detail and complexity of his personality—right down to a speech impediment—may be the strongest argument that such a man did exist. Moses is exceedingly human: weak and strong, brave yet tormented by doubt, a rebel but a faithful follower, a warrior and a saint.

He begins his life as a Hebrew born in Egypt during a time of persecution. Hebrew adults there were forced into slavery: "harsh labor at mortar and bricks." When the burgeoning Israelites became

# Who Were
# Moses and David?

One was a great prophet and teacher who delivered Yahweh's laws to his people. The other was a renowned warrior and king. One was the savior of his people, while the other unified Israel and gave it direction.

**In the reception hall of the Knesset, Israel's parliament in Jerusalem, hang three tapestries created in the 1960s by Jewish artist Marc Chagall. The central tapestry depicts the gathering of Hebrew exiles, with David (left) and Moses in principal roles.**

even more of a problem in Pharaoh's eyes, even an infant's lot became dire: It was decreed that newborn males were to be thrown into the Nile. Moses' mother tried hiding her boy, but after several weeks she grew desperate, and left him by the water's edge. The baby was rescued by Pharaoh's daughter and raised as her son.

Life in Egypt was not bad for Moses, but it was intolerable for his blood kinsmen. One day, Moses saw an Egyptian beating a Hebrew. Moses, believing there were no witnesses about, struck and killed the Egyptian. He fled to the land of Midian, where he met Zipporah, daughter of

Jethro. He and Zipporah married and had two sons, but this was not to be the whole of Moses' family. His clan would encompass all members of all tribes within the Israeli nation.

A bush was aflame, and yet—impossibly—it was not consumed. "Moses! Moses!" A voice was calling from the burning bush. "I have marked well the plight of My people in Egypt and have heeded their outcry . . . I have come down to rescue them from the Egyptians." The voice belonged to Yahweh or, rather, YHWH, a Hebrew word that may have derived from "to be"; it became so holy that it could not be pronounced

# Who Were **Moses** and **David**?

**Working in different media, Chagall rendered David and Bathsheba in oil (1962-63, above) and Moses and the Burning Bush in glass (1962-68, opposite). Born to a poor family in Russia in 1887, the artist was raised in the Hasidic culture and, even after gaining fame in Paris, never forgot his roots: The Chagall museum in Nice is dedicated to "the Biblical Message."**

but only read aloud as *Adonai,* "Lord." Yahweh's plan involved Moses, but Moses was not necessarily willing. "Who am I?" to take on this task. Conquering his fears, he approached Pharaoh and demanded that his people be let go, but he was rebuffed. Moses then told his brother, Aaron, to touch the Nile with his staff, and the river turned to blood. Then the plagues descended and Egypt was overrun by frogs, flies, hail, locusts, "a darkness that can be touched" and other miseries. Yahweh's 10th infliction was to kill all firstborn Egyptian males.

Next: Exodus. On the run, Moses parted the Red Sea (in proper translation, the Sea of Reeds—perhaps Sabkhet el Bardowil, a lagoon on the northeastern shore of the Sinai, not far from the Mediterranean Sea). The Israelites passed safely across the dry land, then turned and watched as Pharaoh's soldiers were engulfed by the inrushing water. Moses' people were free.

In their continued quest for the Promised Land, Yahweh provided for them. Manna fell from heaven when food ran out in the wilderness; Moses drew water from a rock to quench their thirst. In return, Yahweh asked obedience and atop Mount Sinai gave Moses the rules, the commandments—the "ten pearls," as ancient rabbis called them. Although Moses himself would not reach the Promised Land, he pointed the way for his people.

Some two centuries after Moses, the prophet Samuel, with an eye toward uniting the disorganized tribal federation that was the Israelite nation, anointed Saul as king. Saul alternately succeeded and stumbled, was exuberant or depressed, depending on whether he was in or out of the Lord's grace. Tired of Saul's flawed religiosity, God directed Samuel to Bethlehem to seek out a man named Jesse: "I have decided on one of his sons to be king." The chosen one was Jesse's youngest, David, a shepherd boy. Samuel "took the horn of oil and anointed him in the presence of his brothers; and the spirit of the Lord gripped David from that day on [1 Sam. 16:13]."

David entered Saul's service soon after, first as a lyre player retained to assuage the king's despondency, then as a warrior. No one could be found to fight the Philistine Goliath of Gath, a 10-foot-tall mountain of menace—until David. He entered the field of battle with only a sling and stones. Goliath sneered, but David said boldly, "You come against me with sword and spear and javelin; but I come against you in the name of the Lord of Hosts." David's first shot found its mark, the giant fell, and as David took Goliath's sword to behead the man, the Philistine army fled.

David's fame among the Israelites was instant and immense. The tragic Saul now worried that he had a challenger in his midst. The king made attempts on David's life, and David finally fled the court. More than once, he sought refuge among the Philistines, then he and his army were on the move when he received word that Saul had died after a battle at Mount Gilboa. The remnants of Saul's army could not compete with David's increasingly powerful forces, and in about 1000 B.C. the tribal elders, meeting at Hebron, established David as king of Israel. David relocated to Jerusalem, which he named as his capital. In subsequent battles he drove the Philistines back into Philistia, conquered several Canaanite cities and expanded Israel's reach and power. David made Israel great.

Not wanting to fall out of favor with Yahweh, as had Saul, David carefully combined state with church. He saw the symbolism of relocating the sacred Ark of the Covenant, which contained the Ten Commandments, from Kiriathjearim to Jerusalem. He collected dozens of psalms for worship. He stayed loyal to God, and the prophet Nathan said to David, "Your house and your kingship shall ever be secure before you; your throne shall be established forever [2 Sam. 7:16]."

David, like Moses, was only too human—women being his weakness. He married one of Saul's daughters, had a son with each of six wives in Hebron, then took other wives and concubines in Jerusalem. Bathsheba was the wife of one of David's soldiers when she became pregnant by the king, whom she married after her husband's death in battle. God was not pleased with David's behavior, and the infant died. Bathsheba and David had a second son, Solomon, and he was nominated by his father as the royal successor. This was sanctioned by Yahweh. Circa 961 B.C., "David slept with his fathers, and he was buried in the City of David"— having unified a nation.

Is this what Moses surveyed just before he received the word of the Lord? As with much biblical history, this is conjecture; belief is a matter of faith. There is more than one Mount Sinai in the Middle East, including a famous peak on the Sinai Peninsula from which this photograph was taken. There are at least eight places that could have been the setting for the story of Moses and the Ten Commandments.

# In the **Jewish** Holy Land

Throughout the Middle East, temples, tombs and ancient
fortresses mark the passage of prophets and kings.

The first king of Israel reigned for about two decades some 3,000 years ago. Saul was the son of Kish, a prosperous member of the tribe of Benjamin, and was made king by the 12 tribes of Israel. Saul's brilliance lay on the battlefield, where he inspired a largely volunteer army to repeated success against the Philistines. Yet he could not deliver the coup de grâce, and it was on Mount Gilboa, seen here beyond the Valley of Jezreel, that Saul and three of his sons died in combat with the Philistines. In his elegy, Saul's successor, David, said: "The beauty of Israel is slain upon thy high places: how are the mighty fallen!"

Jerusalem's Temple Mount was the site of the First Temple, built by Solomon, as well as the Second Temple, raised by Herod the Great. All that remains from the latter is part of a retaining wall from its courtyard, known as the Western Wall. (Gentiles sometimes call it the Wailing Wall, owing to the lamentations there, but many Jews consider the name undignified.) Note its proximity to the Dome of the Rock.

The traditional King David's tomb (above) is in a nondescript building on Mount Zion in Jerusalem. (There are those, however, who believe that the Zion site may actually be an early Judeo-Christian synagogue.) Left: The Ark of the Covenant, a wooden chest that contained the Ten Commandments, was kept here in Shiloh before it was captured by the Philistines. At right, these steps leading to the Temple Mount were ascended by King David.

At the Dead Sea stands Masada (above). In the first century B.C., Herod the Great
built a fortress atop the mesa, and later, a thousand men, women and children held
out for two years against a Roman army 15 times larger. Masada remains a symbol
of pride for Jews. In 1947 a Bedouin shepherd made a stunning find in the cliffs
of Qumran (opposite): the Dead Sea Scrolls, manuscripts that shed light on rabbinic
Judaism and links between Jewish and early Christian traditions.

# Who Was **Jesus**?

A Jewish carpenter's son born to humble circumstances, he grew to become a charismatic preacher who espoused radical philosophies. His words attracted a handful of followers and then, in the centuries following, billions.

MUSEUM FÜR ANGEWANDTE KUNST, KÖLN

**Hans Memling, born near Frankfurt am Main circa 1430, was a portraitist and painter of Christian imagery; during his career in Brussels and Bruges, he revisited certain crucial episodes in Jesus' life. Of his depictions of Mary with Jesus, the one above, painted between 1470 and 1472, is the most intimate, with no instrument-playing angels in attendance.**

He was descended from Abraham through the line of Isaac, as it extended through David. So says the New Testament of the Christian Bible, which concerns itself with the life of Jesus: born to Mary and Joseph, the Christ, God's son made flesh. His people were from Nazareth, but two Gospel authors are agreed that he was born in Bethlehem. Angels and a shining star signaled that his was a special nativity; still, nothing in Jesus' life presaged the phenomenon that would follow his brief time on earth, which may have been as short as 33 years.

The earthly son of a carpenter, Jesus seemed ready to follow in the family trade but then showed a precocity for philosophy and teaching, lecturing even his elders and senior clerics. If his message offended some, it was alluring to others; he was, in an era crowded with prophets, soothsayers, doomsayers and Zealots, especially charismatic. Jesus' thinking was radical. At a time when there was not only strong-arm rule by kings but also, in the streets, greed, violence and lawlessness, notions of pacifism and charity were alien. The idea of giving one's cloak to a needy stranger—a *brother,* Jesus suggested—did not have much currency in Palestine before he existed. Even religions that would reject him as the Son of God, including Judaism and Islam, would later admire many of his sociological theories. These rules for living were and remain exquisite, and in fact, many of Allah's teachings as rendered by Muhammad some 600 years later are not unlike those of Jesus in their compassion, selflessness and social unorthodoxy.

As Jesus gained followers and notoriety, things

began to be said about him: that he performed miracles, walked on water, fed a multitude with meager rations, raised the dead. In the New Testament, these stories are not presented for their supernatural effect but rather to forward a moral point or to instill faith. They certainly rallied Jesus' disciples, who started whispering, "He's the one." This was dangerous for all concerned.

Jesus, courting fate, went to Jerusalem at a time when his ministry was no longer a secret to the city's hierarchy. With him traveled a small group of loyal apostles—including one who would betray him—and a slightly larger group of camp followers. Tormented, Jesus secluded himself to contemplate what was about to be set in motion. He returned to his friends, telling them during supper that there was a traitor in their midst. This was Judas, who subsequently identified Jesus for local authorities. Jesus was condemned for blasphemy, tortured and then crucified on the hill at Calvary, outside Jerusalem. He

**Memling, who in his lifetime was called "the most skillful painter in the whole of Christendom," gained just and lasting fame. He was often copied, and a debate still rages over how much current Memling is Memling. Most critics feel that at least 20 major works are authentic, and that the artist's reputation is secure based upon that oeuvre. These pages show a copy of a Memling triptych depicting Christ's persecution, crucifixion and resurrection.**

was buried in a rock tomb by Joseph of Arimathea. The New Testament tells of Jesus' resurrection three days later and a direct ascension to heaven, where he and the father, God, await the ultimate judgment day of all mankind.

In the immediate aftermath of Jesus' death, there was no predicting that his cult would survive any longer than the others that were then receiving attention. But his philosophy was so profound, his message so attractive, and his succeeding generations of disciples so determined, that Christianity gained a toehold as a world religion. Then, after a converted Jew named Paul and the first pope, Peter, took the theology to Rome, it slowly rose to become the ruling faith of the empire. It has since fractured and fissured with various orthodoxies and Protestant denominations rejecting the rule of Roman Catholicism, but in the 21st millennium—as Christians measure it—Christianity remains the world's largest religion.

Jesus' people were from Nazareth, a modest, even overlooked village. Jesus performed his first miracle, changing water into wine, nearby. Today, Nazareth, still bucolic in places but with a total population of 72,200, is Israel's largest Arab city.

# In the **Christian** Holy Land

In Bethlehem, Jerusalem and throughout the surrounding hills and valleys, the path and passion of Jesus can be traced.

Was Jesus born
two millennia ago
in a stable or cave in
Bethlehem (left),
a town five miles
south of Jerusalem
in the Judean Hills?
Some doubt this,
thinking Nazareth
more likely for a
Nazarean and noting
that the sanctification
of Bethlehem seems
too convenient a way
to fulfill a prophecy
that the Messiah
would come from
Bethlehem. But a
majority opinion in
the Christian Bible's
New Testament,
and throughout the
Christian world,
is that Bethlehem
is where Jesus' life
and saga began.

The Sea of Galilee—
actually a 64-square-
mile freshwater lake
in a depression of
the Jordan River—
supported several
vibrant cities in Jesus'
day. Five of his 12
disciples were from
villages on the
Galilean shore, and
Mary Magdalene
came from a Galilean
town as well. Jesus
preached here often;
nearby, he delivered
the Sermon on the
Mount ("Blessed are
the meek . . . "). Here,
he turned five loaves
of bread and two fish
into a meal for many.
Jesus calmed Galilee's
waters. He even
walked upon them.

DENIS WAUGH

**From birth to death: In Bethlehem's Church of the Nativity, an ornate star marks the site traditionally regarded as the spot where Jesus was born. In Jerusalem, a Greek Orthodox priest lights a candle and a woman pays obeisance at the door of the Church of the Holy Sepulchre, which honors the place where Christ was crucified.**

RICHARD T. NOWITZ (3)

A ridge in Jerusalem called the Mount of Olives was visited by biblical figures, from the prophet Ezekiel to King David to Jesus. On one slope, in the serene Garden of Gethsemane (above), Jesus was betrayed by Judas. After Jesus' death and subsequent resurrection, he appeared to his disciples on the road to Emmaus, not far away (today, in el-Qubeibeh, left). From atop the mount, the church of St. Mary Magdalene is a grand image set against the ancient city (right).

# Who Was **Muhammad**?

In a volatile age there emerged a serene, strong leader who bequeathed to his people a treatise so moving and wise that it became the bedrock of Islam. Muhammad said he was merely the agent. The Koran was the word of Allah.

**In Islamic art, icons and living things are not to be depicted lest the artist challenge Allah's place or vision. These 16th century Turkish pictures show the infant Muhammad with angels, and (opposite) praying at the Kaaba.**

He was descended from Abraham through Ishmael in a line that included many prophets—but none after him, for he was destined to become the Seal of the Prophets.

Muhammad was born nearly six centuries after another great philosopher, Jesus of Nazareth, spawned a cult that bloomed into a durable religion. As with Jesus, there was little—except perhaps his name, which means "highly praised"—in Muhammad's early years to indicate that this man would found a discipline for the ages. Mecca, a desert city in what is now Saudi Arabia, was a sea of strife in the late 6th century, and when Muhammad's parents died young, the boy was adopted by an uncle. Muslim tradition tells us that Muhammad's heart was infused at an early age with light, love, charity and all manner of pure-heartedness.

The Meccan environment, chaotic religiously as well as sociologically, and dominated by a variety of polytheisms, was not a setting likely to nurture such a character. As a young adult, this mattered little to Muhammad, a benign soul working in the caravan trade who married at age 25. It would be another 15 years before he began preaching in earnest. What happened in the interval is crucial: He went regularly to a cave outside Mecca to contemplate, to question the superstitions of his age and to pray. He wondered about Allah, a supreme god to many Meccans. Eventually, Muhammad became convinced that Allah was the only one—the God. "*La ilaha illa 'llah!*" was the tenet Muhammad brought down from the mount. There is no god but God.

Now came the Night of Power. In the cave, an angel came to Muhammad and charged him to "Proclaim! In the name of thy Lord and Cherisher,

# Who Was **Muhammad**?

**In these illustrations from *Progress of the Prophet*,** Muhammad is visited by the archangel Gabriel; he and his followers are greeted by the Muslims of Yathrib; and, finally, he is visited by the Angel of Death, who escorts him to heaven.

Who created—Created man, out of a clot of congealed blood: Proclaim! And thy Lord Is Most Bountiful—He Who taught the Pen—Taught man that which he knew not [Koran 96:1–5]." So began Muhammad's rendering of the Book, the Koran, the holy narrative of Islam delivered by the angel . . . the word of Allah, by Allah.

Allah would dictate words to Muhammad during the remaining 22 years of the Prophet's life. His lessons, which implored listeners to forsake evil—licentiousness, greed, avarice—certainly did not fall as revelation upon the greater populace; in three years, Muhammad had only a few dozen converts. He, like Jesus before him, was preaching outside the box, and like Jesus in Jerusalem, he got into trouble in Mecca.

He fled, and the year of his flight—622 by

Christian reckoning—is regarded as year zero by Muslims. He went to Yathrib, subsequently called Medinat al-Nabi, "the city of the Prophet" and then, simply, Medina, the city. There, he lived in a humble clay house while continually, through his teachings, commandeering the minds of his new townsfolk. Finally, the great majority of citizenry came to revere its new leader and backed him wholeheartedly when he challenged Mecca for the soul of Arabia. He won, he lost, and then, eight years after he had left Mecca, he returned in ultimate triumph. He immediately forgave the Meccans, and in short order went to the Kaaba, a temple that was said to have been built by Abraham himself. Muhammad rededicated the Kaaba as the holy heart of Islam.

In 632 A.D., he died in Medina. In the next century, Muslim armies washed over Armenia, Iraq, most of North Africa including Egypt and Lebanon, Palestine, Persia, Spain and Syria. Muhammad had given the Arabs a religion, and today it is the second largest in the world.

Completed circa 692, the Dome of the Rock, a rotunda on an octagonal base in Jerusalem, is the oldest extant Muslim shrine. It is from here that Muhammad ascended to heaven at the end of his Night Journey. Nearby are the al-Aqsa Mosque, the Western Wall and the Church of the Holy Sepulchre.

# In the **Muslim** Holy Land

Muhammad's life was lived in two places principally—Mecca and Medina. But as Abraham's descendant, Muhammad is of Canaan, too.

Within the Great Mosque in Mecca is Islam's most sacred shrine, the Kaaba, which all of Islam faces five times a day for prayer. Every Muslim must come here once, circumambulate the Kaaba seven times, then touch and kiss the Black Stone, set in a corner of the Kaaba. In 630, Muhammad removed pagan symbols from the Kaaba, covered here by a black curtain.

In the late 16th century, the Ottoman Sultan Murad III commissioned an illustrated manuscript based on Mustafa Darir's *Siyar-i Nabi,* or *Life of the Prophet,* written two centuries earlier. The massive project resulted in one of the greatest works of Islamic art. Because the story was not considered scripture, the illustrations didn't violate Muslim law (though even with the Prophet's face veiled, some conservatives may be offended). The illustrations on pages 52 through 55 are from the Sultan's commission, as is the one above. In this scene, set in Medina, adherents are at work on a building that will serve as both Muhammad's home and a mosque. The Prophet helps with construction, which utilizes mudbrick and the trunks and leaves of palms. The site was chosen when Muhammad let loose his camel and waited to see where the beast came to rest. Across the years, the mosque has often been enlarged. Today it is a hundred times the size of the original, and 260,000 worshipers may be housed, as in the Friday congregational prayer at right.

The Mosque of the Prophet is second only to Mecca as a sacred place for Muslims, who visit in great numbers each year. Above, the devout depart after the *maghrib*, or evening, prayers. A huge extension of the mosque, finished in 1995, provides air conditioning (opposite) for the hot summer days. Including those who pray outside in an area covered in marble, worshipers can number a million.

On Mount Hira (opposite), outside Mecca, Muhammad received his first revelation from the archangel Gabriel. The Prophet used the cave beneath the white stone for meditation. Above: Muslims believe Adam and Eve met in the Plains of Arafat, in the present day Saudi Arabia. Water cools pilgrims (and trees) in the heat. The Kaaba's Black Stone, right, is the symbol of Allah's covenant with Adam.

# Pilgrims
# Through the Ages

Politics and war may have redrawn boundaries in the Middle East, but holy land has always been homeland, calling to the devout. These pilgrims answered, braving any foe and traveling any distance to pay homage.

For centuries, Jews were on foreign soil in Jerusalem, guests of Muslims, Ottomans or whoever else ruled Palestine. Efforts to reestablish a Jewish nation started up in the late 1800s, about when the photo at left was taken. Above, in 1908, also at the Western Wall.

Christians, visitors in the land of Christ's birth, return to biblical settings to honor their lord and savior. Left: In 1899 a christening in the Jordan River recalls the baptism of Jesus by John the Baptist. Below: a year later, on the road to Jericho. Right: Also in 1900, priests reenact scenes from Christ's passion by carrying a great cross through the Via Dolorosa in Jerusalem.

In 1908, Muslims parade through Jerusalem (left). At the time, the city and indeed all of Palestine was in the hands of the Ottoman Turks, the great majority of whom were followers of Islam. Right: The Dome of the Rock attracted a steady stream of pilgrims a century ago, as it does today. Below: Then as now, Mecca was, of course, the ultimate destination for Muslims. A caravan of Persian pilgrims, bound for the sacred city, establish a camp at the ancient port of Jaffa, which is now part of Israel's largest urban center, Tel Aviv.

# Holy **War**

Whose land is this? In the 20th century, that difficult question was posed, over and over, against the echo of gunfire.

With the city of Jerusalem as a backdrop in January 1948, three armed Arabs scan the Silwan Valley for any Jewish opposition.

Rancor between religions is hardly uncommon, and the history of Jews and Muslims is no exception. Whether the discord stems from religious differences, economic rivalry or, ironically, from a chafing similarity—brother against brother—in today's struggle, a plot of land provides a point of detonation. Because the geography involved is relatively small, it is all too easy for the principals to bump into each other, and in this part of the world, push is invariably followed by shove.

There have been, in years past, many instances of Jews living harmoniously within larger Islamic states. Indeed, these places have generally been considered preferable to enclaves within Christian lands. But seeking shelter as a subordinate culture within a Muslim territory and operating as a separate, powerful state are quite different.

This nation-state, now called Israel, took root in the late 1800s when disenfranchised Russian Jews settled in Palestine, leading to a Zionist tenet that the land was rightfully theirs. The

**At right, in February 1948, terror grips Jerusalem's Ben Yehuda Street after an Arab bomb kills 57 and wounds more than 100. That same year, a ship bearing orphans from Eastern Europe pulls into Haifa. From 1917, when the British wrested Palestine from the Ottomans, to 1948, the number of Jews living in that region increased tenfold.**

inherent problems could not have surprised them; early on, Asher Ginzberg, an influential Zionist, wrote (under the pen name Ahad Haam) that Palestine was too small and bore the challenge of a large native population. Nevertheless, the seemingly perpetual clock of contention had been set in motion.

After World War I, the League of Nations gave Great Britain a mandate over Palestine, which had long been under Ottoman rule. In the preamble to the mandate was the 1917 Balfour Declaration, whereby Britain supported the Jewish effort to secure a homeland in Palestine. But the mandate proved only to be an incubator for tension and flare-ups. After WWII, Britain decided to pass the problem along to the U.N., which in 1947 called for dividing the region into two separate states. Zionists were pleased, at least momentarily, but Palestinians and Arabs were appalled by the emergence of a Western-like domain in their midst. They responded with guns: Just one day after

**The relatively new United Nations shouldered the onerous task of monitoring the 1949 truce. The U.N. also provided many refugees with aid and housing, as here in December 1953 at a school for Palestinian refugees near Jericho.**

Israel declared itself a nation in May 1948, Arab forces from Egypt, Syria, Jordan, Lebanon and Iraq attacked. Intense fighting alternated with truces until, in early '49, an armistice was reached with all but Iraq. For the Israelis, the fighting resulted in the destruction of important agricultural areas. For the Arabs, it was a far worse nightmare. They had been humiliated by the army of a new country, which ended up gaining land, including West Jerusalem. Even worse, in what is still referred to as "the disaster," hundreds of thousands of Palestinians fled their homes and ended up in an area controlled by Jordan—the West Bank. The refugee debacle has ever since been a tinderbox in the Middle East.

During the next few years there were intermittent clashes, but the truce somehow held until 1956, when Egypt nationalized the Suez Canal. Israel felt menaced by the Soviet-backed buildup of Egyptian forces, led by President Gamal Abdel Nasser. In October, Israel's Moshe Dayan led a sortie into the Sinai Peninsula. Britain and France, in concert with the Israelis, joined in two days later. Finally the U.N.—at the behest of the Americans and Soviets—halted the fighting, but not before Israel had taken the Gaza Strip. Bowing to international pressure, Israel relinquished Sinai and Gaza in '57 while retaining vital access to the Gulf of Aqaba. For his part, Nasser cleverly parlayed defeat into victory by consolidating the Muslim world in his battle against Zionism.

Fighting was relatively light for several years; then, in 1964, after Israel had nearly completed a project to divert water from the Jordan River to the Negev Desert, Syria started work on a similar operation near the river's headwaters. This facility would seriously diminish the Israeli water supply, so Israel promptly destroyed the facility, and tempers on both sides grew shorter and shorter.

In 1967, after a string of skirmishes and provocations—for example, the Soviets told Syria that the Israelis were massing troops near its border, which probably wasn't so—matters again came to

a head. Israel, infuriated that Egypt had sealed off the Gulf of Aqaba and feeling threatened by its troops in the Sinai, launched a preemptive air strike against the Soviet-built Egyptian air force, much of which never left the ground. Within three hours, most of Egypt's planes and air bases were demolished. It was June 5, the beginning of what is known by Israelis as the Six-Day War, and called by Arabs the Setback. By the time the U.N. secured a cease-fire, the Israeli victory, a masterpiece of thrusts and counterthrusts, had stunned the world.

The Star of David now flew over Gaza, Sinai, the strategically located Golan Heights and the West Bank of the Jordan River, including East Jerusalem. The latter was of the utmost importance. For Israel, East Jerusalem—the Old City, with its holy sites—is at the crux of Judaism and is simply not a point for negotiation. For the Palestinians, their historic territorial claims and the holy sites there make it a point on

These photos were taken in 1967 during the crucial Six-Day War. At top left, Israeli infantrymen on the Via Dolorosa in Jerusalem's Old City advance block by block. Bottom, a soldier kisses the Western Wall. The photograph at right was taken near the Nile by a low-flying Israeli pilot. As the shadow of his Mirage jet approaches, four Egyptians take what cover they can.

**A wounded Israeli soldier (opposite) receives treatment and a kind word from a bloodied buddy at an aid station during the Yom Kippur War in 1973. Above, Israeli soldiers fire a 175mm cannon in the Golan Heights. This war severely damaged the Israeli economy and led to the resignation of Prime Minister Golda Meir.**

which they simply will not compromise.

Saddled with another frustrating defeat, the Arab world began to embrace the three-year-old Palestine Liberation Organization. With their armies wrecked, Arab states began siphoning funds to the PLO. Thus were financed forays into Israel and its occupied lands. Israel responded with actions against the organization's host countries, Jordan and Lebanon. Nevertheless, the PLO had used the Six-Day War as a springboard to the realm of international powerbrokering.

In 1970, Nasser was succeeded by Anwar Sadat, who grew increasingly disturbed by diplomatic failures to alter Israel's dominance in the region. Sadat entered into negotiations with Syrian President Hafiz Assad. On October 6, 1973, with the support of six other Arab nations, Egypt and Syria launched surprise attacks. It was Yom Kippur, the most sacred of Jewish holy days, as well as the 10th day of Ramadan, the anniversary of a famed battle fought by the prophet Muhammad. The Israelis, caught off-guard, had to petition the U.S. for help. With its massive dependence on oil, America didn't want to exacerbate

relations with Arab oil-producing states, but when it was learned that the Soviets were supplying matériel to Egypt and Syria, President Richard Nixon ordered an airlift of weapons to Israel "to maintain a balance of forces and achieve stability in the Middle East."

In the end, the result was, once again, the same. After initial losses, Israel emerged victorious and annexed more land, which it later ceded as a result of U.S. pressure. But the Yom Kippur War opened the way for diplomatic talks that came to fruition in 1979 with the Camp David Accords, whereby Israel returned the Sinai Peninsula to Egypt, which in turn recognized the right of Israel to exist.

It was a grand achievement, but the habitual hostilities were not so easily vanquished. In 1982, Israel, trying to wipe out the PLO, invaded Lebanon, which had been harboring the terrorist group. PLO guerrillas were routed but merely found other sites from which to unleash their hostilities.

The late '80s gave rise to a development that, with hindsight, seems inevitable. The Palestinian

CATHERINE LEROY/SIPA

Israel went all out in its effort to destroy the PLO in Lebanon in 1982. Above: Beirut under fire. The Israelis managed to drive Yasir Arafat to Tunisia but ended up in a three-year quagmire. Below: the funeral of a teenage Jewish girl at a West Bank settlement in 1987. Opposite, in '88, the *intifadeh*.

ALLAN TANNENBAUM

people themselves, boiling over after two decades of Israeli occupation—and abetted by Hamas and others—launched an *intifadeh,* an uprising that involved violence, demonstrations, strikes and boycotts of Israeli goods. The televised images of Palestinians hurling stones at the heavily armed Israeli soldiers provided an interesting counterpoint to the David and Goliath tale in the Old Testament—as the Palestinians were no doubt aware.

Other accords would follow, notably the Oslo and Wye pacts, but the bloodletting continues. In a land where religion and politics have taken the form of impregnable alloys, where fervent people strive desperately after sovereignty and self-determination, the symbols, the methods and the land itself have intertwined in an endless tapestry of zealous self-righteousness. If the images coming from Israel and the West Bank during the past several years seem freshly horrifying, the news is nothing new.

ALFRED YAGHOBZADEH/SIPA

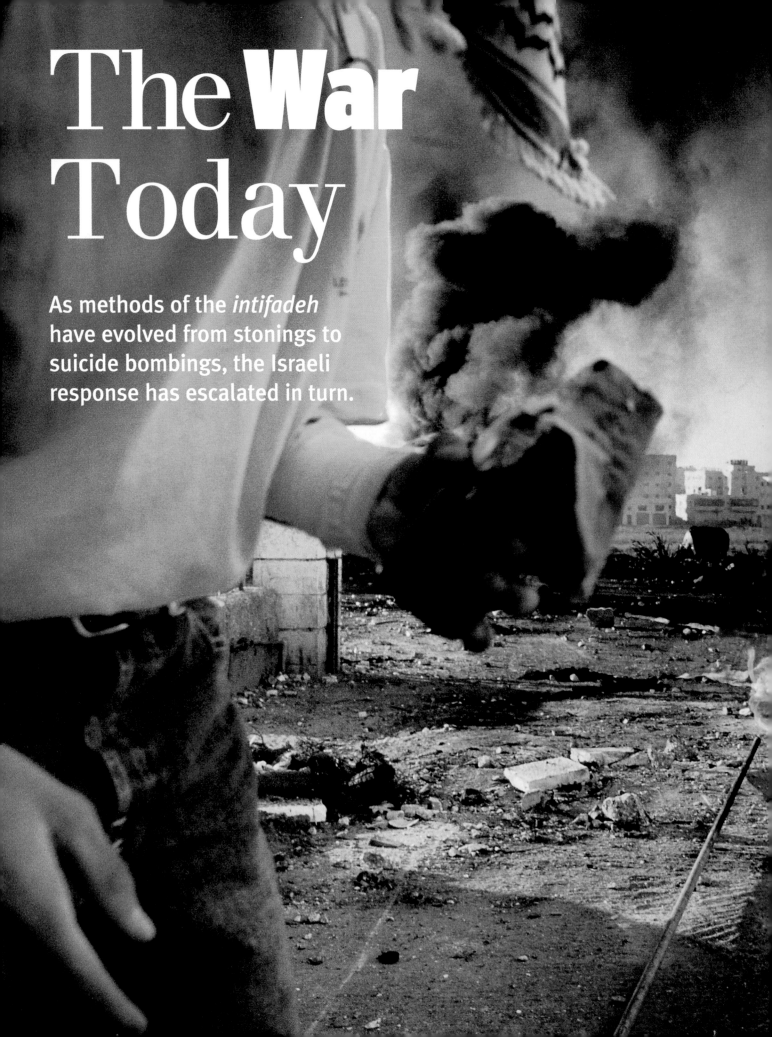

# The War Today

As methods of the *intifadeh* have evolved from stonings to suicide bombings, the Israeli response has escalated in turn.

In the fall of 2000, former Israeli Defense Minister Ariel Sharon's trip to the Temple Mount—known by Muslims, who worship at a mosque on the site, as Haram al-Sharif—was seen by some as politically provocative. Violence in Jerusalem spread to cities like Ramallah, where a Palestinian hurls a Molotov cocktail.

In June 2002, a Palestinian woman in Gaza City, on the Gaza Strip, cautiously peers around the side of a house at an Israeli tank. Nearby lies the Jewish Netzarim settlement, one of about 150 in the West Bank, Golan Heights and Gaza that have sprung up since 1967. They are a wellspring of unrest.

In the not-distant past, there was a ray of hope. Under 1993's Oslo Accords, Israel and the PLO agreed to work for "interdependence," in which Palestine, with self-rule in the Gaza Strip and the West Bank, would be seen as a "partner" in the region, not an "inferior." Then, as ever, things fell apart.

In 1996, bombings by Islamic militants killed dozens, and when Israel opened a tourist tunnel near the al-Aqsa Mosque in Jerusalem, some Palestinians, sensing an attempt to extend sovereignty over a disputed area, took to the streets. More than 50 Palestinians and a dozen Israelis were slain. Another relative lull was followed in 2000 by the area's worst violence in 30 years when, in the week after Sharon's visit to the Temple Mount/Haram al-Sharif, 70 were killed and 1,800 injured.

In the first decade of this century, the main Palestinian method of attack in the *intifadeh* became suicide bombing, and the world looked on horrified as men, women and children were killed in explosions on buses, in cafes and at schools. Some Islamic imams, hoping to stop the carnage, pointed to the Koran and said the bombings violated the teachings of Muhammad, who condemned suicide. The argument in defense of the tactic viewed the bombings as acts of martyrdom. With cultures and theological interpretations clashing, the war raged on.

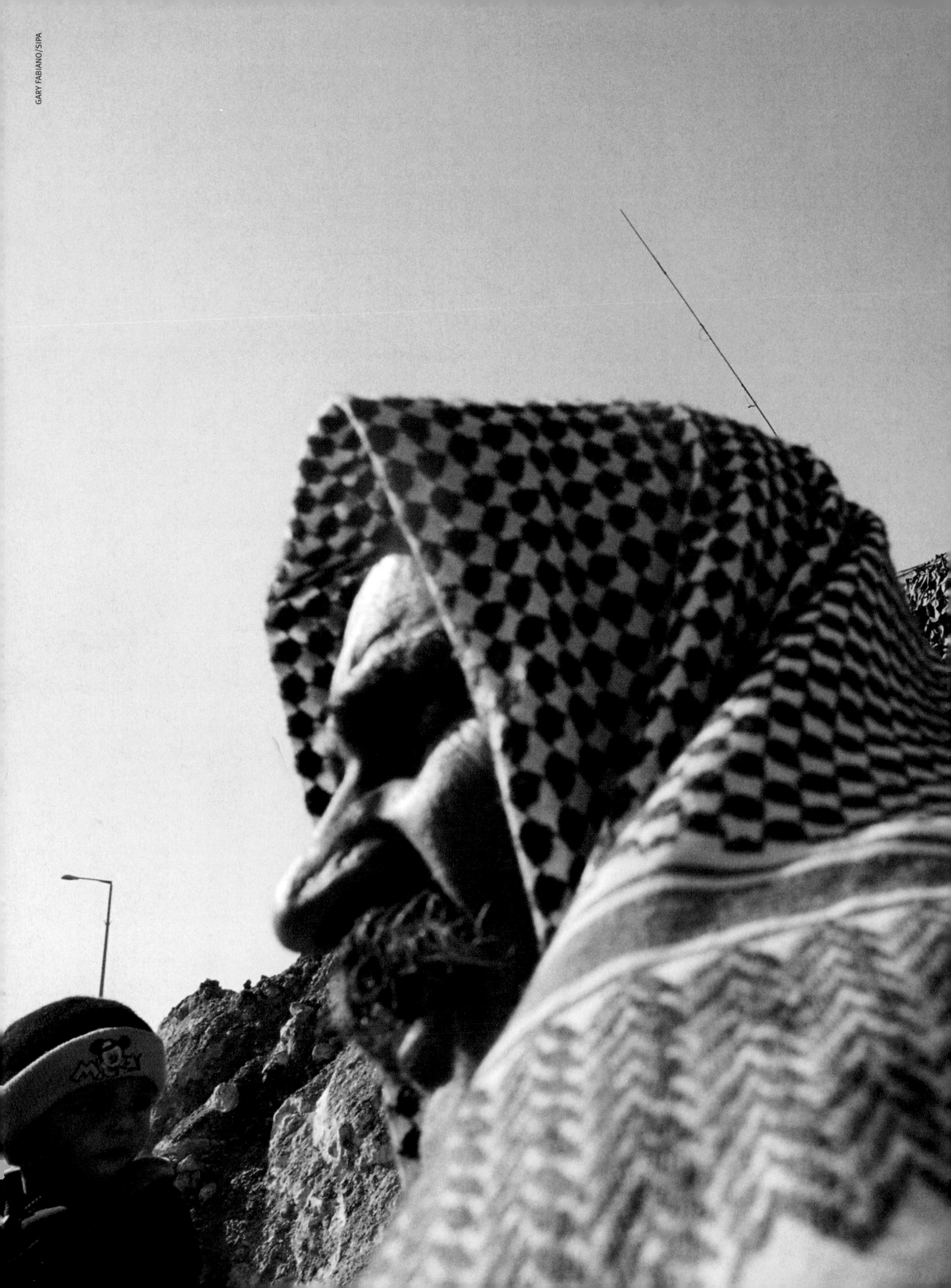

GARY FABIANO/SIPA

An Israeli Defense Force soldier at the Kalandia checkpoint in Palestine surveys the traffic passing from the West Bank town of Ramallah into Jerusalem. For the Israelis, checkpoints are a necessary cog in the never-ending effort to impede the movements of dangerous individuals. To the Palestinians, they are yet one more indignity.

With its citizenry continually subjected to suicide bombings and other forms of terrorism, the government of Israel has responded in a variety of ways, including house-to-house searches. Here, in a refugee camp in the West Bank town of Tulkarem, a Palestinian woman stands by as an Israeli soldier climbs through her bedroom window in search of militants or weapons. Later, loudspeakers demand that all males between the ages of 15 and 45 report for interrogation.

DAVID SILVERMAN/GETTY

The second *intifadeh* has been significantly more violent as Palestinians have increasingly turned to suicide bombings. In June 2001, however, it was a rock cast by a Palestinian that struck the fatal blow against five-month-old Yehuda Shoham, who had been riding in his father's car. (Left, the child's funeral.) Many people have questioned how such devoutly religious people can justify suicide bombing. What about the Koran? While it usually teaches benevolence, the book also sometimes encourages a fight. In the 22nd chapter of the Koran, it states, "To those against whom war is made, permission is given to fight," referring specifically to "those who have been expelled from their homes . . . for no cause except that they say, 'Our Lord is Allah.'"

It is a conflict that drags on and on and on, a source of grief for an untold many. Here, relatives provide what solace they can to the sister of Wael Khweitar, a 27-year-old Palestinian soldier who was also a physician. He was killed in an Israeli raid on the Gaza Strip. Menace, even death, daily prowls the byways of these troubled holy lands.

DAMIR SAGOLJ/REUTERS/LANDOV

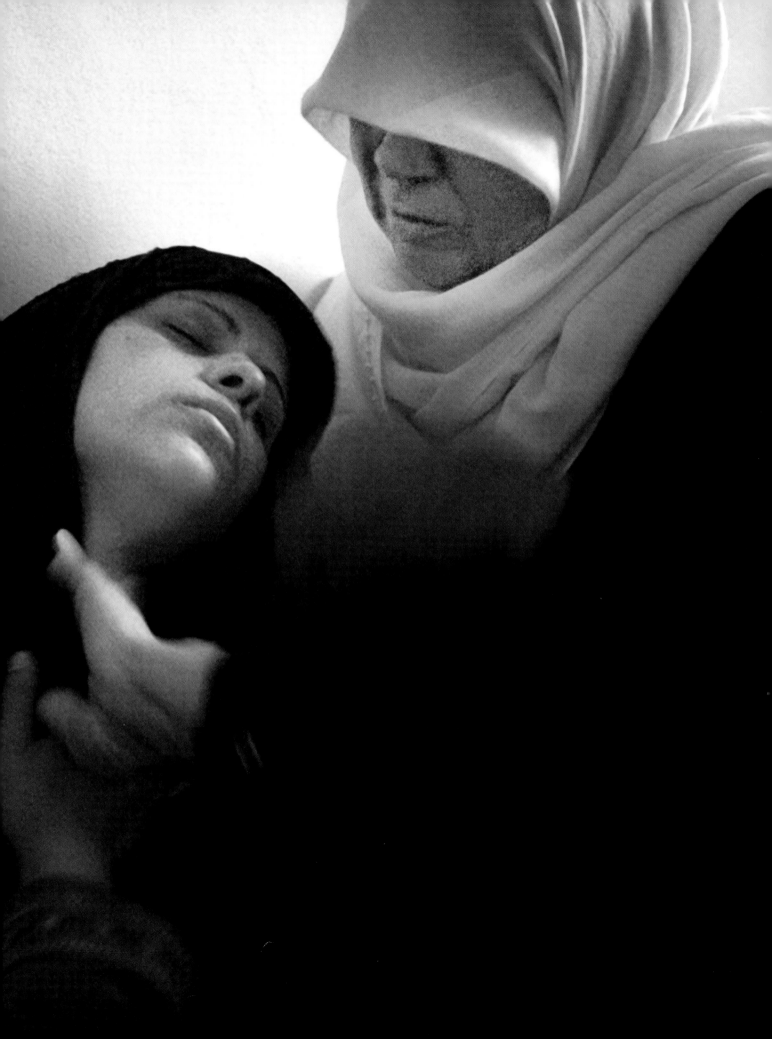

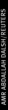

# The Aftermath
# of **Arab Spring**

It was never one revolution but several, and therein lay a problem.
Each situation would be different. In some places, the people's
will prevailed. In others, repression was instant and war followed.
One thing was clear almost everywhere: This was not over.

On June 29, 2012, fireworks explode as tens of thousands of supporters of Muslim Brotherhood candidate, and president-elect, Mohamed Morsy gather at Tahrir square in Cairo. On this day, Morsy takes an informal oath of office, defying the generals once in service to Mubarak who, despite Morsy's recent victory at the polls, are trying to limit his power. The generals ultimately bend to the will of the people, though they remain very much a presence. But nonetheless, quite suddenly Egypt, a linchpin in the region, looks much different than it did only two years earlier.

It began well in advance of the spring of 2011 and continues today and will tomorrow, with consequences uncertain. If the compass of the term *Arab Spring* is inexact, so is the connotation, as we have pointed out in our introduction to this book. Spring alludes to sunshine and flowers, to rebirth and renaissance. These were elements of Arab Spring, to be sure, but so were violence and recrimination and a fierce determination, in some instances, to hold on to power. The killing of Chris Stevens, the situation in Syria today: nothing springlike about these things.

From a Western vantage at the outset, the latest uprisings in the Middle East recalled for some the imagined romance of the 1960s, or the 1770s, or the fall of the Berlin Wall. But for others (and just as quickly), they begged a question: What does this mean going forth? What might Libya look like after Muammar Gadhafi? Egypt after Hosni Mubarak? Will the war in Syria prove intractable?

For Israelis, the question, What does this mean going forth?, was paramount: If we are to be surrounded by Arabia, as is evident, what constitutes survival? Will long-term peace ever be in prospect? There remains, in 2012, no certain answer.

The attitude of the United States toward the holy land—as opposed to simply our interest in the oil resources of the Middle East—came into play. A democratic nation supports and encourages democratic principles, and so, by and large, the U.S. supported the efforts of Arab peoples to take back their countries from dictators and tyrants. Our politicians, pundits and populace cheered when on January 14, 2011, President Zine el-Abidine Ben Ali, in charge of Tunisia for 23 years, fled to Saudi Arabia following a month

What has happened in Egypt has been emblematic, and since Egypt is such a signpost nation, events have been watched for all the glories and risks of Arab Spring—optimistic rebellion, vengeful retaliation, vox populi, the rise of Islamic influence. Scenes from the drama, starting opposite, left: On June 17, 2012, voters check their names at a polling station in Cairo. Election results lead to the first freely elected Egyptian president, the Islamist Mohamed Morsy, who waves to supporters on June 29 in Tahrir Square (opposite, right), surrounded by members of his presidential guard. Below: Same place, same period, a young girl waves an Egyptian flag during a Muslim Brotherhood sit-in protesting the military's desperate maneuvering to retain power.

ALEX MAJOLI/MAGNUM

**In a Tunisian cafe on January 18, 2011, there is relative calm as, on a daily basis outside, police and demonstrators clash in riots. Opposite: Several months later in Tunis, women ride a train, their faces reflecting the continuing tensions. Demonstrations in Tunisia occurred early in the Arab Spring— in fact, well before spring, in late 2010— and inspired other uprisings, including those in Egypt, Algeria, Yemen, Jordan, Bahrain, Iraq, Mauritania, Pakistan, Libya and Syria.**

of protests that grew more violent by the day. Within a month, the forever president of Egypt, Hosni Mubarak, resigned and left the country in military hands until a general election could be held—an election that, the following year, illuminated the strength of the Muslim Brotherhood. On March 15, 2011, the king of Bahrain, Hamid bin Isa al-Khalifa, declared a state of emergency as his troops battled protesters. On August 22, Libyan rebels entered Tripoli. In October, they found and killed Gadhafi. And in the meantime: President Ali Abdullah Saleh of Yemen had fled (in June) to Saudi Arabia after being injured in an attack on his palace; thousands of Syrians had fled to Turkey (also in June, and throughout the summer) as government troops began their crackdown (now nearly two years old) on all manner of revolt; more than 100 people were killed in July 2011 in a Syrian army tank raid on the city of Hama, where dissension was rampant—a signal that death, even the slaughter of innocents, would be a consequence of continued dissent. As the autumn of 2012 approached, with thousands of protesters already dead or injured—there are

no reliable estimates because the worst atrocities are thought to be as yet undiscovered, but 25,000 fatalities seems a conservative guess, the majority of victims being civilians—Syria was still aflame and the United States, with an election season, a wounded economy, the continuing war in Afghanistan and other concerns front and center, was hoping to stay absent from the fray. Then, on September 11, the U.S. consulate in Benghazi, Libya, was attacked and Ambassador Chris Stevens, who had supported the rebels in their fight against Gadhafi, was killed along with three associates. No one on the ground could be absent from the fray.

What, then, does *Arab Spring* mean? So far: a populist revolt with much loss of life, with some successes, and with still-unresolved battles being fought. What it will all mean years hence, in a holy land where religion has always been a predominate issue, is to be determined.

This is, as we have seen, a millennia-old history. It has not been resolved by the events of the last many months, and it is not going to be summed up by tomorrow morning's headlines.

MOISES SAMAN/MAGNUM

Scenes from Libya as Gadhafi falls. Below: A soldier on a mermaid-shaped sofa in the entrance of the home of Gadhafi's daughter Aisha. Bottom: Libyan women in October 2011 meet with counterparts from Benghazi to discuss the upcoming conference on women now scheduled for mid-November in Tripoli. Right: On June 7, 2011, armed guards stand inside the house of Yemeni tribal leader Sadiq al-Ahmar in Sanaa. Revolts against the government had begun in January of that year, and intensified into violence. Yemen is illustrative of just how problematic everything is—or can become—in the region. Of its 24 million citizens, most are Islamic, but of the Muslim population 53 percent are of the Sunni faction (largely in the south and southeast), and 45 percent are Shiite. Before any external quarrels are addressed, internal divisions dominate.

JAMES PALMER/POLARIS

GORAN TOMASEVIC/REUTERS

The terrible situation in Syria in 2012, counterclockwise from left: On July 25, a young girl in pink stands amidst the rubble on a street in Homs, routinely referred to as a rebel stronghold and therefore brutally besieged by government forces, with civilians often the victims; on August 16, members of the Idrees family and their friends in Buwaydah prepare to bury two Free Syrian Army soldiers who have been killed fighting the Syrian army; a Free Syrian Army fighter fires his sniper rifle in Aleppo on August 14; and finally, under cover of darkness along the Turkish-Syrian border in Hatay Province, traffickers working the exodus smuggle a family across the Orontes River to a relative version of safety. In the first year of the current fighting, perhaps 11,000 Syrians fled their country and were living in refugee camps along the Turkish border; in August of 2012, as many as 100,000 fled to Turkey, Lebanon, Jordan and elsewhere. In September, Turkey declared Syria a terrorist state. If the Syrian government so much as blinked, it went unnoticed.

Two different Bibles and the Koran are the blocks upon which these religions rest. History is continually written and rewritten—violence ebbs and then it flows—but finally the faithful must return to the page, to the word of the Lord.

E.R. DEGGINGER/PHOTO RESEARCHERS

## The Hebrew Bible

Written by divinely inspired authors between two and three millennia ago, this is the sacred scripture of Judaism. It is made up of three parts. The first is Torah—or Pentateuch, or "Law"—which sets forth religious and social rules, tells the story of the creation and describes the Lord's covenant with Israel, the Exodus from Egypt, and the Hebrew people's arrival in the Promised Land. Nevi'im ("Prophets") is the Israeli history in Palestine, filled not only with prophecies but with wars and heroes—principal among the latter, David. Ketuvim ("Writings") includes meditations on evil and death, as well as psalms and praises of Israel's covenant with God. The word "Bible" is derived from the Greek *Biblia* (the Book) and has no precise translation in Hebrew; Jews call their sacred volume Tanakh, an acronym for Torah, Nevi'im and Ketuvim. The Torah seen here was found on an archaeological expedition and now resides at Drew University in New Jersey.

# The **Books** Endure

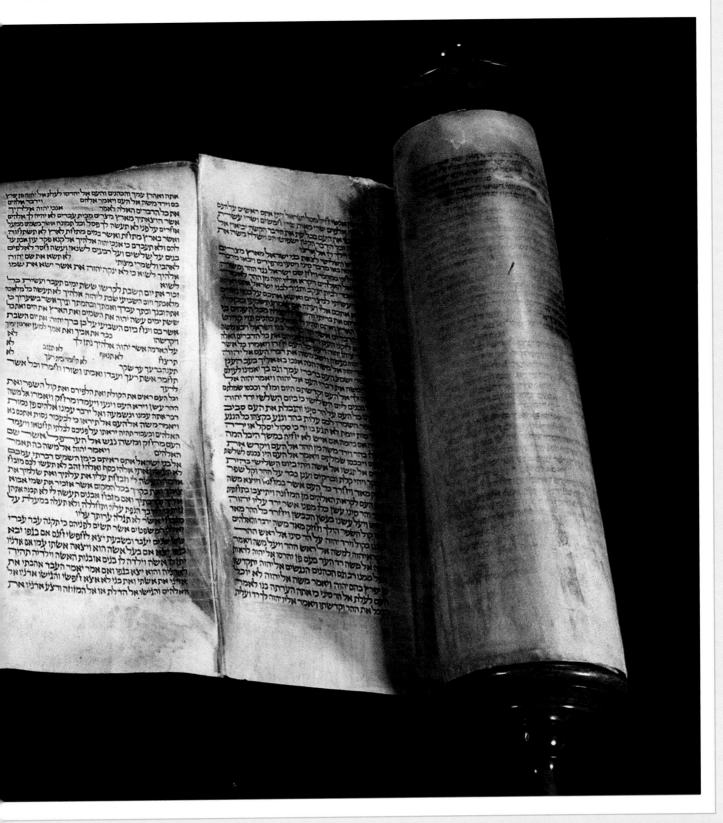

## The Christian Bible

It is often said that the Old Testament of the Christian Bible equates with the entirety of the Hebrew Bible, but this is not the case. When the early Christians were assembling their book in the first century after Christ's crucifixion, they accepted the Jewish view of history as truth—with reservations. Working from a Greek translation of the Jewish Bible rather than from the Hebrew text, they incorporated nuanced changes that would prove crucial (for instance, the mother of the Messiah would be "a young woman," said the Hebrew word *almah*, but "a virgin," stipulated the Greek *parthenos*). The Christian Bible, seen here as printed by Gutenberg in 1455, reordered chapters and ignored or diminished some episodes sacred to Jews. And it added a New Testament, whose 27 books constituted a far shorter narrative than that of the Old, but which changed the entire message: Christ was the Messiah, so all that came before was leading to *him*, not to a still-prophesied savior.

## The Koran

Muhammad could neither read nor write, so he listened to Allah's words, then passed them along to his people orally. The stories and laws were not recorded in book form until after his death. In the Koran, which means "the Recitation," much of Jewish tradition is confirmed by Allah, as is the greatness of Jesus as a prophet (he foresees his successor, Muhammad). But Jesus as the son of God: This is blasphemy. And the Christian doctrine of a Holy Trinity—Father, Son and Holy Spirit—is seen as polytheistic (a very serious point, since Muhammad was converting an Arab world that was, before his rise, largely polytheistic). As with the Tanakh and the Bible, the Koran, a centuries-old version of which is seen here, stresses obedience to God (Allah) and sorrow for one's sins. It warns of Allah's final judgment and speaks of heaven and hell. As with the Old Testament, there is violence, sometimes meted out in Allah's name, but the Koran more often urges mercy and compassion.

# In the **Heart** of the Matter

Here, in the Old City of Jerusalem: a square mile of holiness. The golden Dome of the Rock glistens, with the al-Aqsa Mosque adjacent (to the right, in the photograph). The Western Wall is visible just below the mosque. And the Church of the Holy Sepulchre's black dome dominates the lower foreground.